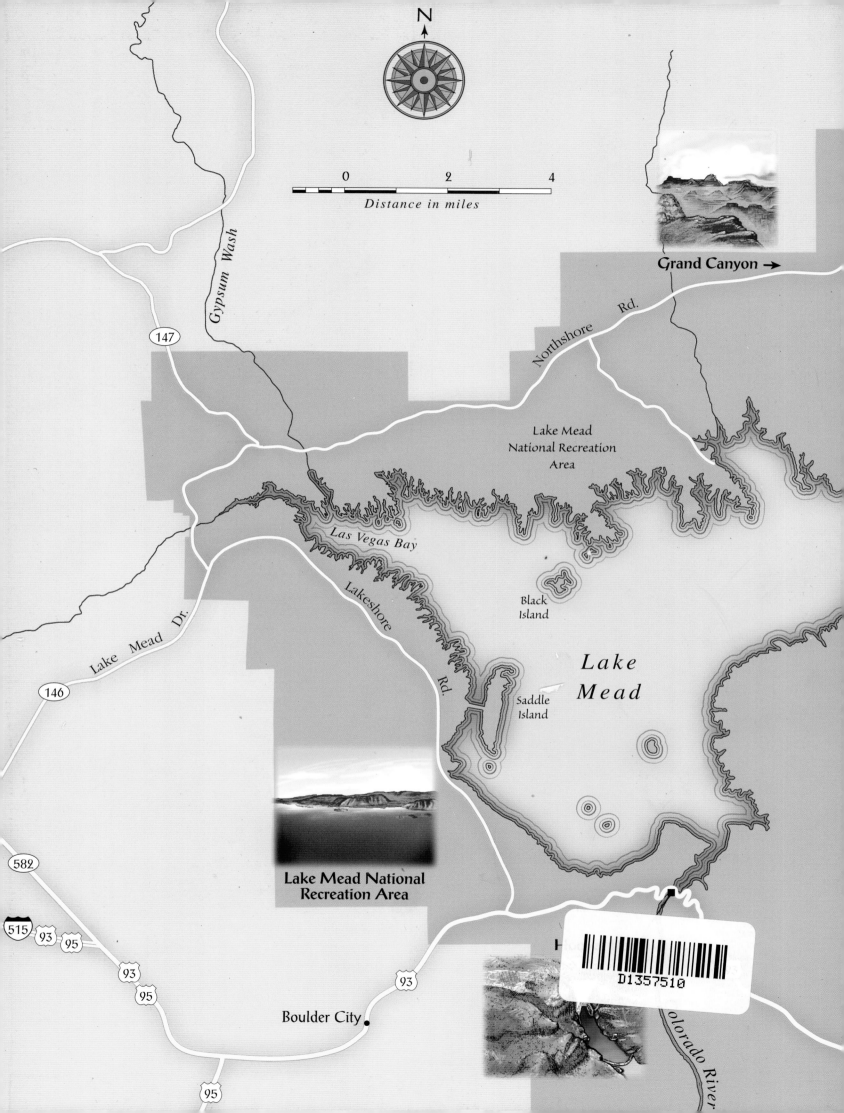

N

0   2   4

Distance in miles

Gypsum Wash

147

Grand Canyon →

Northshore   Rd.

Lake Mead
National Recreation
Area

Las Vegas Bay

Lakeshore   Rd.

Black
Island

*Lake
Mead*

Lake   Mead   Dr.

146

Saddle
Island

582

**Lake Mead National
Recreation Area**

515   93   95

93

95

93

95

93

Boulder City •

H

Colorado River

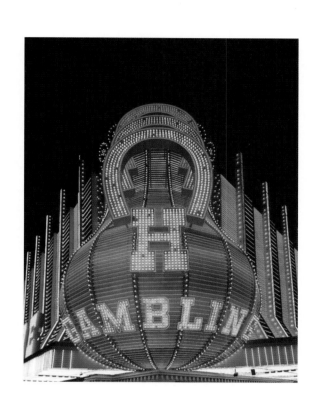

CAROL M. HIGHSMITH AND TED LANDPHAIR

LAS VEGAS

A PHOTOGRAPHIC TOUR

CRESCENT BOOKS

NEW YORK

FRONT COVER: Looking at the gaudy procession of resort megacasinos, it's hard to imagine the days when "the Strip," a two-lane highway to Los Angeles, was dotted with tourist courts and billboards. BACK COVER: Las Vegas action movies rarely feature the city's slots parlors, such as this room under the Tropicana's leaded-glass casino ceiling, but they draw loyal crowds. PAGE 1: Binion's Horseshoe Club opened on Fremont Street downtown in 1951. It later turned its entire façade into spectacular walls of light. PAGES 2–3: At many a dusk and dawn, nature provides its own Las Vegas light show.

This 2003 edition is published by Crescent Books,
an imprint of Random House Value Publishing,
a division of Random House, Inc., New York.

Crescent is a registered trademark and the colophon is
a trademark of Random House, Inc.

Random House
New York • Toronto • London • Sydney • Auckland
www.randomhouse.com

Printed and bound in China

A catalog record for this title is available
from the Library of Congress.

ISBN: 0-517-22055-5

8 7 6 5 4 3 2

Designed by Robert L. Wiser, Archetype Press, Inc.,
Washington, D.C.

All photographs by Carol M. Highsmith unless otherwise credited: map by XNR Productions, page 5; "Baccarat" oil painting by LeRoy Neiman, page 6 (© LeRoy Neiman, Inc., Knoedler Publishing, LLC, New York); Steven Cutler (curator, Casino Legends Hall of Fame at the Tropicana, Las Vegas), pages 8–10, 12–20; Las Vegas Convention and Visitors Authority, pages 11, 21; Alex Sauer/Reuters/Getty Images, page 61; "Art of the Motorcycle" exhibition (© The Solomon R. Guggenheim Foundation, New York), page 71.

THE AUTHORS WISH TO THANK THE FOLLOWING FOR THEIR GENEROUS ASSISTANCE AND HOSPITALITY IN CONNECTION WITH THE COMPLETION OF THIS BOOK:

Holiday Inn Express, Henderson, Nevada

Wayne Bernath, publicist for Lance Burton, Le Cage, and the Crazy Girls

Richard Hooker, Senior Cultural Program Specialist, City of Las Vegas

Lisa Keim, Public Relations Manager, Tropicana

Yvonne Lewis and Mike Ensign, Mandalay Resort Group

Frank H. Lieberman, National Publicist; and Philip Misiura, General Manager, Siegfried & Roy

Robert Manzanares, Public Relations Coordinator, Caesars Palace

Karen Moore, Paul Anka Productions

Andrea Primo, Sales and Marketing Manager, Henderson Convention Center

Tom Schaus, Operations Manager, Sundance Helicopters

Bernie Yuman, Bernie Yuman Management

Sandy Zanella, Public Relations Specialist, MGM Mirage

The authors salute Deanna DeMatteo, creator and owner of the Las Vegas Strip History website, which contains invaluable nuggets of information on the evolution of the area.

And we commend the City of Las Vegas and the Young Electric Sign Co. for preserving so many classic Las Vegas outdoor signs that had been discarded and could easily have disappeared into the mists of nostalgia. Instead, some are displayed in the city's new Neon Museum, while others have been remounted on city streets.

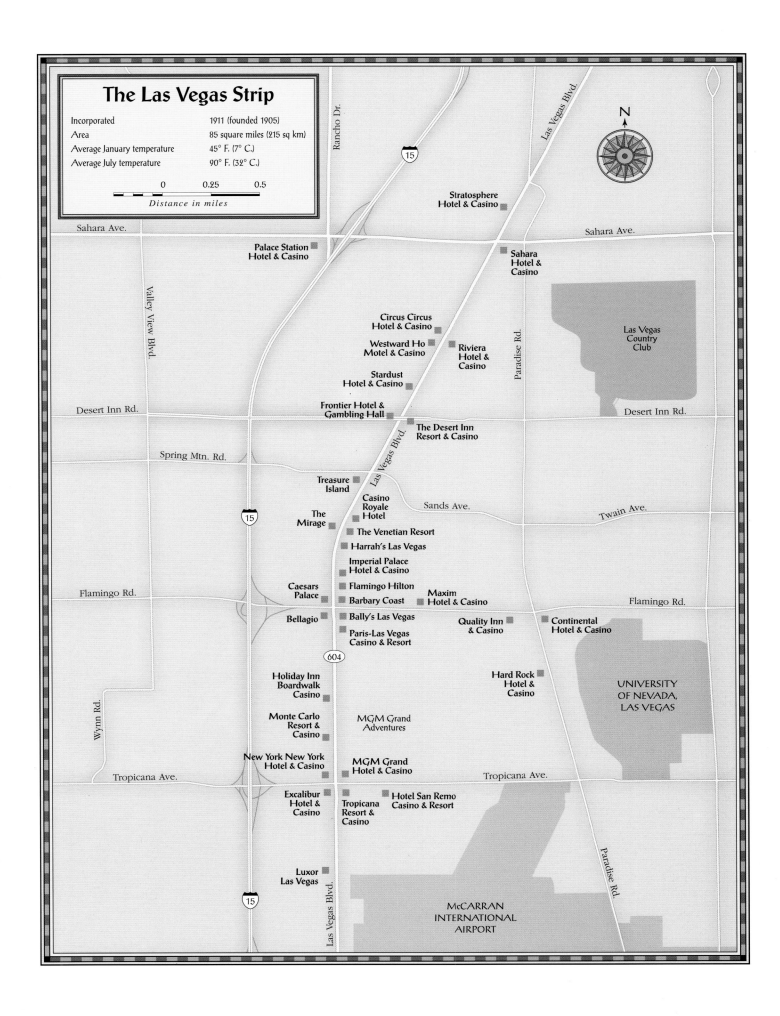

The Las Vegas Strip

Incorporated   1911 (founded 1905)
Area   85 square miles (215 sq km)
Average January temperature   45° F. (7° C.)
Average July temperature   90° F. (32° C.)

0   0.25   0.5
Distance in miles

N

Rancho Dr.

Las Vegas Blvd.

15

Stratosphere
Hotel & Casino

Sahara Ave.

Sahara Ave.

Palace Station
Hotel & Casino

Sahara
Hotel &
Casino

Valley View Blvd.

Paradise Rd.

Las Vegas
Country
Club

Circus Circus
Hotel & Casino

Westward Ho
Motel & Casino

Riviera
Hotel &
Casino

Stardust
Hotel & Casino

Frontier Hotel &
Gambling Hall

Desert Inn Rd.

Desert Inn Rd.

The Desert Inn
Resort & Casino

Spring Mtn. Rd.

Las Vegas Blvd.

Treasure
Island

Casino
Royale
Hotel

Sands Ave.

Twain Ave.

15

The
Mirage

The Venetian Resort

Harrah's Las Vegas

Imperial Palace
Hotel & Casino

Caesars
Palace

Flamingo Hilton

Maxim
Hotel & Casino

Flamingo Rd.

Barbary Coast

Flamingo Rd.

Bellagio

Bally's Las Vegas

Quality Inn
& Casino

Continental
Hotel & Casino

Paris-Las Vegas
Casino & Resort

604

Holiday Inn
Boardwalk
Casino

Hard Rock
Hotel &
Casino

UNIVERSITY
OF NEVADA,
LAS VEGAS

Monte Carlo
Resort &
Casino

MGM Grand
Adventures

Wynn Rd.

New York New York
Hotel & Casino

MGM Grand
Hotel & Casino

Tropicana Ave.

Tropicana Ave.

Excalibur
Hotel &
Casino

Hotel San Remo
Casino & Resort

Tropicana
Resort &
Casino

Paradise Rd.

Luxor
Las Vegas

Las Vegas Blvd.

15

McCARRAN
INTERNATIONAL
AIRPORT

BACK ABOUT 1940, WITH THE NATION GIRDING FOR WAR, NOBODY thought to set up a time-lapse camera on rip-roaring Fremont Street's casino row in Las Vegas, or on the two roads heading south out of town. One, Boulder Highway, snaked down to what was then called Boulder Dam, open just four years, twenty miles away. The other was Route 91, the Los Angeles Highway, an extension of Las Vegas Boulevard knifing into the inhospitable desert. Even its first three-mile stretch outside city limits—which would one day sprout into the world-famous Las Vegas Strip of mind-boggling themed resorts—was then just a two-lane, unlighted, and unremarkable road, lined with sagebrush, a few billboards, and assorted gas stations. In the chocolate-colored hills between the two highways glowed the embers of a grimy little government town alongside magnesium and titanium deposits that workers would soon turn into fighter jets. These places, along with downtown's saloon-style casinos, ordinary banks, dry cleaners, grocery stores, and trailer parks where footloose dealers and cocktail waitresses made a home were the sum and substance of "Sin City." Nevada had legalized gambling in 1931, but the heart of Nevada gaming was up north in Reno and at clubs around Lake Tahoe, not Vegas's boozy "Glitter Gulch."

In 1829 Spanish traders had stumbled upon a patch of green they called Las Vegas—"the Meadows"—around a spring in Paiute country near the parched Mojave Desert trail from New Mexico to California. Western explorer John C. Frémont, for whom Vegas's main street would one day be named, traipsed through in 1844. But nobody stayed until eleven years later, when thirty Mormon missionaries dispatched by Brigham Young built an adobe fort, planted fruit trees, and scratched for lead in Potosi Mountain. Disheartened by incessant Indian raids, the Mormons departed in 1858, and nobody much paid attention to the place until the railroad from Los Angeles reached it in 1904. The building of Boulder Dam to the south stirred up a ruckus in town in the 1930s, but Las Vegas remained little more than a gaudy diversion on the long haul between Salt Lake City and L.A. As of 1940, eight thousand people and uncounted critters endured life there.

Now roll that film ahead a bit more than sixty years to the early 2000s, when more than 1.5 million people live in the Valley. The metropolitan area's astonishing 83-percent growth rate in the 1990s led the nation, while the country as a whole recorded a 13-percent population increase. Fueling this economic explosion: disposable dollars dropped by more than thirty-five million visitors a year, a forgiving business-tax structure and absence of a state income tax, a pleasant climate in the nine months outside the beastly summertime, and plenty of high-paying jobs.

Suppose someone *had* hooked up time-lapse cameras along Fremont Street's sawdust-on-the-floor clubs downtown and on the two southbound roads out of town in 1940—and somehow kept them running? Saving that scrawny desert road to Los Angeles for last, here's what they would reveal:

Boulder Highway slowly turned to seed, its lively motels and vibrant neon signs that once coaxed travelers off the road now decrepit, hanging on, or gone. Fremont Street nosedived too, for a time. The beer-and-bluejeans crowd stayed and played downtown, while eye-popping magical palaces along the emerging Strip outside town siphoned off more and more tourists. Yet downtown came back rollicking. In the 1990s more than $1 billion was spent on a facelift, most notably featuring the world's largest electric signboard—a canopy of 2.2 million colored lights and 218 enormous speakers arrayed above four blocks of Fremont Street. Each nighttime

The Strip was a nearly empty highway in 1941 when Los Angeles hotelier Tom Hull built the bungalow-style El Rancho Vegas with an inviting pool and neon-lit windmill. It burned down in 1960 and was not rebuilt.

hour through midnight these days, the glittering casino façades dim as this "Fremont Street Experience" erupts in a Cecil B. De Mille-scale, computer-generated sound and light show. Even "Vegas Vic," that rascally, winking neon legend from the old Pioneer Club, shines brightly again, and so does his saucy girlfriend "Vegas Vicki" across the street above Sassy Sally's.

The dusty government townsite down among the mineral-rich hills slowly evolved into the City of Henderson, named for a U.S. senator from Nevada who, it is said, never set foot in the place. There are still some boxy workers' homes and gritty Henderson neighborhoods. But obscure Henderson exploded into a Vegas bedroom community of subdivisions and golf courses, tripling in size in the last decade of the twentieth century. Henderson raced past two hundred thousand in population, stunning the state by overtaking Reno as Nevada's second city. The trigger may have been the day in the 1960s when Hank Greenspun won his lawsuit against Howard Hughes. Greenspun, maverick publisher of the Las Vegas *Sun*, carped at the billionaire recluse over one issue or another, so Hughes huffily pulled his casinos' advertising from the *Sun*. The courts agreed this was restraint of trade, and Hughes paid the judgment against him in the form of forlorn desert property that he valued at one hundred dollars an acre. The land looked scrubby and uninviting, but it offered hilltop views of burgeoning Las Vegas and a breeze or two. Greenspun turned it into Green Valley, the heart of booming Henderson and one of the most upscale planned communities in the world, boasting a sizeable share of the Valley's more than sixty world-class golf courses. In 2000 *Money* magazine named Henderson the nation's top retirement destination.

And then there is that dusty road to Los Angeles.

As the 1940s progressed, motels like the Tumbleweed and the Last Frontier with seventy to

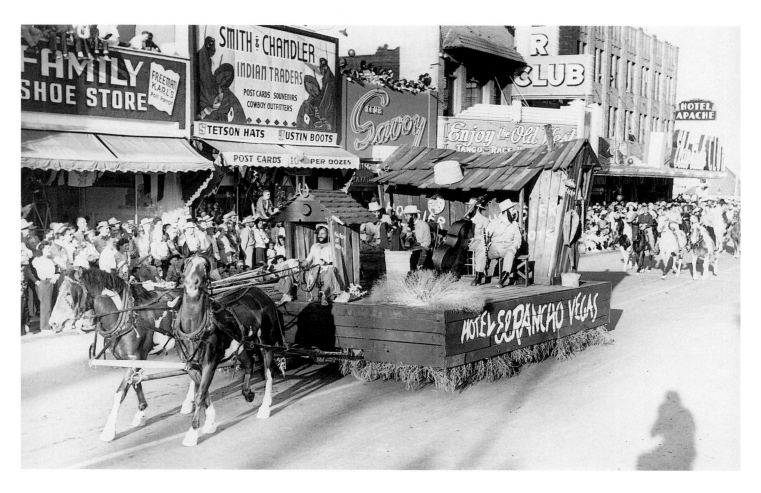

one hundred tourist rooms, modest casinos, and intimate clubs, began to pop up every half mile or so; most, like upheld the Vegas tradition by selecting a western name and motif. One that did not, the "Fabulous Flamingo," offered just 105 rooms. To appreciate the stunning transformation to come along the old road, today's Flamingo Las Vegas on the same site boasts more than thirty-six hundred rooms.

The sixty-three-room, dude-ranch-style El Rancho Vegas, built by California hotelier Thomas Hull, had been the first motel-casino to venture past city limits and onto the barren L.A. Highway in 1941. Its windmill tower, spacious pool, and Chuck Wagon Buffet became landmarks. In the showroom the El Rancho Dice Girls pranced in ample costumes with hats the shape of dice. The little resort lasted until 1960, when its casino, restaurant, and lounge burned to the ground in a raging fire, with no loss of life. Although properties like the Stardust, Riviera, and Sahara had opened by that time, nobody rebuilt El Rancho or put another behemoth resort on the property. Its grounds remained vacant into the twenty-first century.

Las Vegas has a penchant for reinventing itself to suit the times or trend, and the first overhaul began in the 1950s along this highway—which was beginning to be called "the Strip." Deanna DeMatteo's exhaustive Las Vegas Strip History website reports that Guy McAfee, a local vice squad commander, coined the name; he said it reminded him of the sophisticated clubs he had seen along Los Angeles's Sunset Strip in the 1930s. A parade of desert-theme properties popped up in a wave of resort construction. First was the Desert Inn, which occupied the prime location at the cross street of the same name until demolition crews blew it to rubble in 2000. Then followed the Sahara—the "Jewel of the Desert"—across from El Rancho; the Sands, where the Venetian stands today; and the Dunes, on the site of today's Bellagio. Despite our

Las Vegas staged its first "Helldorado" parade and rodeo in 1944. By 1996, its last year, the homespun event, geared to locals, seemed small-town corny amid Las Vegas's explosion of theme-park-style megaresorts.

romantic visions of desert splendor, all were humble, low-slung affairs with a handful of guest rooms. Even the newest, Aladdin, which debuted in 1966, opened with just 335 rooms. Showrooms stole the thunder, enticing gamblers away from downtown. Ray Bolger and Connie Francis at the Aladdin; Edgar Bergen and Charlie McCarthy at the Desert Inn; Danny Thomas, Frank Sinatra, and Sinatra's "Rat Pack" at the Sands; Maurice Chevalier at the Dunes; and Teresa Brewer and Victor Borge at the Sahara were among the headliners. Lavish production companies like Harold Minsky's *Folies International* at the Sands and Lou Walters's *Folies Bergere* at the Tropicana—which opened in 1957 almost three miles down the highway—began to set sensational standards that other resorts hustled to copy.

Pity traveling families, however. Shopping in the Strip's early days was confined to hotel gift shops and small strip centers, and parents had a hard time finding any place beyond the pool to entertain children. There was a Wild West arcade or two—even a *faux* ghost town right on the Strip—and plenty of all-you-can-eat family buffets to choose from. But that was about it for the under-eighteen crowd. All that changed in 1966 with the opening of Caesars Palace— which offered *three* immense pools and an extensive "Forum" arcade of upscale shops. Then came Circus Circus Casino in 1968, which four years later expanded into a family resort hotel chock full of clowns, acrobats, and even an elephant. The first MGM Grand, with movieland-theme theaters, a day-care center, bowling alley, and "youth entertainment center" featuring early video games, followed in 1973. Caesars and the MGM Grand enticed patrons not only with gaming, showrooms, and sumptuous accommodations but also with championship boxing matches and other headline-grabbing events. On New Year's Eve, 1967, for instance,

The action in Las Vegas in 1943 was on Fremont Street, where western themes and artistic signs caught the traveler's eye. This was neon's heyday, before massive light-bulb arrays turned the desert night into day.

daredevil Evil Knievel nearly died when his motorcycle crashed on a landing ramp after he soared over Caesars' fountain. These properties, and newer blockbuster resorts to come, soon consigned most old motel-casinos to history's dustbin. Together, in a second re-invention of Las Vegas into a legitimate resort destination, they boasted more than nine thousand high-rise rooms at their openings. Older properties like the Flamingo, Aladdin, and Sands kept construction cranes busy trying to keep up.

But Las Vegas had seen nothing yet.

The 1990s and first years of the new millennium saw Vegas refashion itself yet again, borrowing the mystique of faraway places in fanciful properties that shot up like Spring daffodils along the Strip. Below Tropicana Avenue, where only the modest resort of that name, the old Hacienda casino motel, and tinier motels kept company with the cacti, three stupendous complexes—Excalibur, the Luxor, and the Mandalay Bay, offering ten thousand rooms among them—materialized in the 1990s. Excalibur took Las Vegas visitors on a journey to King Arthur's Court, and the pyramid-shaped Luxor to ancient Egypt. Other improbable "destinations" appeared just up the Strip: Hollywood at the new MGM Grand, the Big Apple at New York New York, Paris and Monte Carlo at resorts with those names, the canals of Venice at the Venetian, and Lake Como country at the Bellagio. Classic Vegas venues were obliterated or extensively renovated to make room for these and other megaliths: the Sands, replaced by the Venetian; the Marina, by the MGM Grand; the little Desert Rose Motel disappeared in favor of the Monte Carlo; the Lone Palm Motel and a worn-out trailer park were succeeded by New York New York; the old MGM Grand was supplanted by Bally's; the Dunes became the Bellagio; and the Castaways gave way to the Mirage.

What's Las Vegas without showgirls? These were the pre-topless days when flamboyant costumes, a chorus line of well-turned legs, some honky-tonk piano, and a slightly risqué comedian were enough of a show.

In the early 1960s much of the Strip was still barren desert. There was not yet a Caesars Palace to the south of the Dunes (foreground), and nothing below the Flamingo, across the road.

Seemingly overnight, the Strip became a gaudy entity unto itself, apart from Las Vegas and dramatically different in character. Here there are only two scales: Big and Bigger hotels, signs, showroom acts, atriums, thrill rides, slots jackpots, even buffets. At the turn of the century Las Vegas boasted *all ten* of the largest hotels in America, and fourteen of the top fifteen. The quality of those properties had skyrocketed from the city's rough-and-tumble days as well. In 2000, when Treasure Island was awarded AAA's "Four Diamond rating," Las Vegas passed even New York and Chicago to lead the nation with seventeen thousand Four Diamond-rated rooms. Surveys now show that *shopping*, not gambling, is the No. 1 visitor attraction in Las Vegas. The Venetian's Grand Canal Shoppes, for instance, attract more than fifty thousand visitors a day—more people than tour the Louvre in Paris. And Vegas's culinary reputation soared, too, from its ninety-nine-cent-buffet days. In 2000 AAA bestowed its coveted Five Diamond Award upon two Vegas restaurants: Picasso at the Bellagio and Renoir's at the Mirage.

For the first time ever in Sin City, non-gaming activities—rooms, meals, shows, rides, shopping arcades—are bringing in more revenue than the gambling tables. Most are promoted by dazzling electronic billboards. According to the Nevada Power utility, the electricity needed to illuminate just the outdoor signs on the Las Vegas Strip could electrify an entire city of twenty-five thousand. Vegas casino and resort owners just laughed during the summer of 2001 when neighboring California, facing brownouts, suggested that Vegas might want to dim its lights in the dead of night to help the regional power grid. Their city without lights, Las Vegas responded in effect, would be like Scotland without moors, the Alps without snow, or Bali without the sea. Besides, half the power needed for southern Nevada was generated right there, and there it would stay.

Vegas has dimmed its casino lights, and paused most gambling action—albeit briefly—at least four times: in 1963 after the assassination of President John F. Kennedy; when Vegas troopers Dean Martin and Frank Sinatra died in 1995 and 1998, respectively; and out of respect for those who perished in the September 11, 2001 terrorist attacks in New York; Washington, D.C.; and Pennsylvania.

Not every venerable Strip property was razed to make room for a colossus with a dream theme. Some classic properties like the New Frontier (founded as the Last Frontier in 1942), the Flamingo (1946), the Sahara (1952), the Riviera (1955), the Tropicana (1957), the Stardust (1958), Caesars Palace (1966), and the Holiday Inn Boardwalk (born as the Holiday Casino in 1969) kept their names, upgraded their façades and facilities, and competed by emphasizing their family atmosphere, showroom acts, casino attributes, and even their pools. Imaginative, even garish, signs blinked everywhere. "The architecture of persuasion," Robert Venturi and two co-writers describe these shimmering advertising extravaganzas in *Learning from Las Vegas*, a remarkable study of Vegas's architectural symbolism. The Strip's gargantuan properties sit so far apart, the book points out, that getting people into the parking lot is the paramount challenge. Because of the distances, exuberant light displays, not subtle neon, were chosen to catch the eyes of passersby.

One property that exemplifies Las Vegas's capacity for reinventing itself is the Aladdin, whose colorful story includes a heyday, underworld ties, fiscal collapse and closure, and a remarkable reincarnation. The Aladdin opened in 1966 on the east side of Las Vegas Boulevard between Tropicana Avenue and Flamingo Road after owner Milton Prell renovated a Tudor-

Swimming pools would become commonplace in the 1950s motel boom across America, but they were a welcome amenity in Las Vegas's scorching summer heat. No children splashed in this one: note the floating gaming tables.

The 1952 Moroccan-themed Sahara replaced the Club Bingo parlor across the street from the El Rancho in 1952. It proclaimed itself "the hotel that made Las Vegas the entertainment capital of the world!"

style motel called the King's Crown Tallyho. Prell kept the Tudor façades on the motel's 335 rooms, built a showroom called the "Baghdad Theater," added a casino, and put up a fifteen-story sign out front topped by a caricature of Aladdin's lamp. A year later the casino resort made world headlines when it hosted Elvis Presley's wedding. Over the years the property added a second Arabian-themed showroom, the Sinbad Lounge; installed *Minsky's Burlesque* at the Baghdad Theater; and added a nineteen-floor guest tower. In a bizarre turn of events, the hotel was closed—but for just a few hours—in 1979 after its general manager and casino boss were sent to jail by a federal jury in Detroit, Michigan, for allowing shadow owners to control the Aladdin. A U.S. District Court judge reopened the resort quickly because, he said, prolonged closure would ruin hundreds of innocent resort employees.

In January 1986 the Aladdin was closed again, this time not for hours but for fifteen months, because of Mob ties and evidence of cash skimming. During that period it was purchased by a wealthy Japanese of Korean descent, Ginji Yashuda, an international high roller and former race-car driver. Yashuda kept eighty employees on the payroll during the months the Aladdin was shuttered. It reopened, but under a financial cloud. When Yashuda refused to tell the Nevada Gaming Commission the source of foreign loans, the commission revoked his license. Yashuda died of cancer in 1989. Rumors flew that Frank Sinatra or Wayne Newton or Donald Trump was buying the resort, but it was run by the bankruptcy court for three years. Its Bedouin theme all but forgotten, the Aladdin, then under the ownership of a New York real estate developer, featured top rock and country artists and the "Country Tonite" musical in its showrooms. Facing insurmountable competition from the new megatheme resorts around it, the Aladdin announced in 1997 it would join the crowd, demolishing the old

hotel and replacing it with a new $1.2-billion resort that would keep the Aladdin name. The imploded resort fell early on the morning of April 27, 1998, its giant Aladdin's lamps preserved in the city's Neon Boneyard. "In a city that tends to implode its history, the Aladdin is unique," Nevada State Museum curator Frank Wright is quoted as saying, "Aladdin is the first resort to rebuild and retain its original name. That link to our city's rich past is hard to find in Las Vegas." In 2000 the new Aladdin opened with 2,567 rooms and a renovated, seven-thousand-seat Theatre of the Performing Arts.

Las Vegas has had its idiosyncratic episodes, like the days in the early 1950s that the federal government conducted more than one hundred nuclear tests in the flats beyond Mount Charleston, just sixty-five miles from town. Casino resorts packed picnic lunches for their guests to carry into the desert, as close to the blasts as they could get. Hotel bars served "atomic cocktails" upon their return, lounges dressed up their showgirls in "mushroom clouds," and the local Sears stores sold out of Geiger counters. A fuzzy color photo from the time, showing a bright red cloud boiling skyward in the distance beyond Glitter Gulch, looks like a retouch job. But it's all too real. "Downwinders" in southern Utah—farther from the blast site than Las Vegas—would later document an alarming increase in cancer deaths in the years following the Nevada testing. Perhaps because of the transient nature of Las Vegas, no provable correlation between the explosions and any health consequences was ever confirmed.

And, of course, Las Vegans love to talk weddings: three million of them as of July 3, 2001, when Alberto Recio and Marlen Rodriguez of Miami, Florida, exchanged vows in Spanish at the We've Only Just Begun Wedding Chapel at the Imperial Palace Hotel and Casino. Want to get married at two in the morning? Vegas is your place. A Martha Stewart Wedding; April Fool's

Suits, ties, and cocktail gowns were standard attire among an earlier generation of Las Vegas gamblers. This photograph was meant to accentuate Strip casinos' elegance, as differentiated from the rustic, western ambience of downtown clubs.

Wedding Special; an intergalactic, gangster, Harley cycle, or beach-party theme? How about getting married on horseback, while sky-diving, or in a hot-air balloon? You've come to the right place. Do you want "Elvis" to walk the bride down the aisle and sing romantic ballads? That's a natural, because the town has never forgotten the fuss over Elvis Presley and Priscilla Beaulieu's nuptials in 1967. Johnny Weissmuller, Betty Grable, Joan Crawford, Paul Newman and Joanne Woodward, Mary Tyler Moore, Bette Midler, Bruce Willis and Demi Moore, Richard Gere and Cindy Crawford, and Billy Bob Thornton all got married in a local casino or chapel.

In another Las Vegas reinvention of sorts, giant hospitality corporations call the tune at most properties today. But it was not always thus. The fantasyland that is Las Vegas is a monument to unforgettable characters and risk-takers. Here's a rogue's gallery:

Benny Binion, founder of the downtown Horseshoe Club, was a hero to the "little guy." A Texas bootlegger, Binion helped turn Depression-era Dallas, awash in oil money, into a veritable gambling den. Convicted of one murder, cleared of a second, suspected in a number of other rub-outs of rival operators, "The Cowboy" was encouraged to leave town by a reform administration. He landed in Las Vegas in 1951, opened Binion's Horseshoe Club, where he served Texas-style chili to patrons, introduced poker as a Vegas table game—later sponsoring national poker tournaments—and raised the payout on craps and other games so that even small-town visitors could have a shot at big payouts. At the Horseshoe, Binion even displayed one million dollars, in ten-thousand-dollar bills, for all to see and long for. His son Jack told the Las Vegas *Review-Journal* that his father was the first in town to pick up high rollers from the airport in limousines, first to offer free drinks to slots players, and first to lay a carpet in a Las Vegas casino. "If you wanta get rich," Binion, who died in 1989 at age eighty-five, told his controller, "make little people feel like big people." A bronze statue of Bennie Binion—in Stetson hat astride a cowboy pony—stands in downtown Las Vegas today.

Benjamin "Bugsy" Siegel, a killer and partner of Mob boss Meyer Lansky, built the Strip's first true resort, or what Siegel called "carpet joint," as distinguished from the cowboy haunts downtown. The radiant Flamingo flaunted its flaming-pink neon sign and flamingo statuary but sequestered Siegel's bullet-proof, steel-reinforced office; trap doors; and escape tunnels. Siegel, who had the looks, ego, and comely girlfriends of a matinee idol, was blown away in Hollywood—presumably by another wiseguy after the oft-delayed, over-budget Flamingo opened in 1946. This inextricably tied Las Vegas to Mob influences that U.S. Senator Estes Kefauver, Attorney General Robert F. Kennedy, Las Vegas FBI agent-in-charge Joe Yablonsky, and a handful of courageous journalists would further expose. Bugsy Siegel may have met his fate because of cost overruns or the skimming of Flamingo construction funds, but just as likely his associates grew weary of his fondness for flashbulbs.

Howard Hughes made his name as a billionaire businessman, aviation pioneer, Hollywood producer, and drug-addled recluse long before he arrived in Las Vegas. The addiction and reclusiveness stemmed in part from his treatment for agonizing pain endured after he crashed airplanes throughout Southern California. In his healthier, swashbuckling days the dashing entrepreneur often gambled and picked up showgirls in Las Vegas. On Thanksgiving Day, 1966, he was

Well!! Cheapskate Jack Benny, an occasional headliner and pal of several Vegas entertainers, had his own penny slot machine at the Tropicana Club. Getting him to part with that copper coin, though, took some doing.

THIS MACHINE RESERVED FOR Jack Benny

Frank Sinatra called the "Rat Pack" of late-night carousers at the Sands Copa Room his "Clan." The singers and swingers included (left to right) Peter Lawford, Sinatra, Dean Martin, Sammy Davis Jr., and Joey Bishop.

smuggled into town in a private Pullman car and carried in a litter to the Desert Inn's penthouse, where he would live in the shadows while he began buying Vegas casinos and land. Before he was done, Hughes owned the Desert Inn, the Sands, Castaways, the New Frontier, the Landmark, and the Silver Slipper. So bizarre and clandestine were his operations that the FBI and the state's own governor, Paul Laxalt, whose career Hughes had helped underwrite, wondered if Hughes were really alive. According to *The Money and the Power*, Sally Denton and Roger Morris's scathing book about the shadier chapters of Las Vegas's past, Laxalt was reassured by telephone calls from someone who sounded like Howard Hughes. But the governor—and the world at large—never actually laid eyes on the demented tycoon. In 1970, Hughes was spirited out of Las Vegas to the Bahamas, never to return. Shriveled to ninety-three pounds, his body covered with bedsores and needle marks, his fingernails curled beneath him, Hughes died in a private airplane, flying over Mexico in 1976.

Another aviator and airline executive, *Kerkor "Kirk" Kerkorian,* made his first fortune ferrying military cargo around the world and gamblers to Las Vegas from Los Angeles. A suave, publicity-shy gambler, Kerkorian bought a piece of the Dunes in 1955. But his land deals proved more lucrative. He acquired empty property across from the Flamingo in mid-Strip for less than $1 million, sold it to Caesars Palace for $5 million six years later, and, for $15 million, bought the Flamingo itself to learn the resort business. Then he launched his first megaresort: the $60-million International off the Strip—instantly the world's largest hotel at 1,519 rooms—which Barbra Streisand and Elvis Presley helped open in 1969. Kerkorian owned the International for a year, selling it to the Hilton Corporation while he planned another dream resort. In 1973 Kerkorian, who had taken over MGM Studios in Hollywood, opened the MGM Grand, inspired

*By switching instru-
ments in a Riviera
Hotel publicity photo,
it was hoped some of
Liberace's Vegas magic
would rub off on Elvis
Presley. "The King"
had bombed in
his debut at the New
Frontier in 1956.*

by the MGM film "Grand Hotel," on the site of the old Bonanza Motel and Casino on the south-east corner of the Strip and Flamingo Road in Las Vegas. On November 21, 1980, the name MGM Grand became synonymous with catastrophe when eighty-five people died in a colos-sal fire. Kerkorian rebuilt it, but, tarred with the stigma of the fire, it floundered, and Kerkorian sold it to Bally Entertainment Corporation for $550 million in 1985. He later bought the Desert Inn, the Sands, and the Marina and attached the MGM name to each of them. The Marina was shuttered in 1990, and the "new" MGM Grand, yet another "world's largest hotel" with more than five thousand rooms, opened in its place three years later. MGM Grand Hotels and an-other investor brought the skyline of "Manhattan" to Las Vegas in 1997 with the opening of New York New York. At age eighty-two, Kerkorian orchestrated MGM Grand's takeover of Mirage Resorts properties in 2000. At that moment the son of Fresno, California, fruit peddlers had an ownership stake in the MGM Grand, New York New York, the Mirage, the Bellagio, and Trea-sure Island on the Strip; the Golden Nugget in downtown Las Vegas; and Beau Rivage, a resort on the Mississippi Gulf Coast.

Like Kirk Kerkorian, another Las Vegas business baron, *William Bennett,* has generally avoided the limelight. A wealthy Arizona furniture-chain owner, he moved to northern Nevada in the 1960s to streamline the business practices of Del Webb's casino operations. His customer-friendly but bottom-line sensibilities were soon put to work behind the scenes at the Mint, bathed in hot-pink lights and neon in downtown Vegas, and at the Sahara on the Strip. In 1974, Bennett and a partner bought Circus Circus, where they established a profitable "midway" of games and other amusements. The partners also bought and made cash cows of casinos in Laughlin, down in Nevada's "point," south of Hoover Dam. With some of the profits, Bennett and his associates at Circus Circus Enterprises created two of the Strip's most audacious fantasy resorts—the medieval-themed Excalibur in 1990, and the Egyptian-inspired Luxor in 1993. Bennett retired a year later—reportedly $700 million richer. He and a partner, Ralph Englestad, owner of the mid-Strip Imperial Palace, then embarked on a remarkable venture north of town. They created the sixteen-hundred-acre Las Vegas Motor Speedway, which opened in 1996 with an Indy Racing League event. The $200-million Speedway, which Bennett and Englestad sold two years later, has been called racing's "crown jewel" because that one facility includes *twenty* different racing circuits for everything from NASCAR stock-car races to drag racing. Although Bennett publicly insisted he knows nothing about racing, he was quick to capitalize on the sport's popularity by incorporating NASCAR themes into the café, looping roller coaster, and "virtual racing center" of the Sahara casino resort, which he spent $100 million renovating.

Bob Stupak had no fancy pedigree. A high-school gambler, pool hustler, and streetcorner bookie in his hometown of Pittsburgh, Stupak tried his hand at singing under the stage name "Bobby Star" at clubs in various Pennsylvania and Ohio steel towns. But he made most of his living in the 1960s selling discount coupon books in the Pittsburgh area and later, improbably, in Australia. Stupak, who had visited Las Vegas and played in Benny Binion's poker tournaments, moved to town in 1971. He advertised himself as an "Australian businessman" looking for investments. They would include a cocktail lounge and a piece of land at the southern end of downtown, just above Sahara Avenue, where the Las Vegas Strip begins. Stupak turned the property into "Bob Stupak's World Famous Million Dollar Historic Gambling Museum and World's Biggest Jackpot." The museum, which was also an operating casino loaded with gimmicks like a $50,0000 payout on a nickel slot machine, burned down in 1974. In 1978, he opened "Bob Stupak's Vegas World," a one-hundred-room miniresort on the site of the burned-out casino museum. Its casino was popular among serious players, room rates were reasonable, and by 1982 Vegas World had added a twenty-four-story, 339-room tower festooned in neon. By now a certified Las Vegas celebrity, driving around town in his "rocket car" modeled after the neon logo of his resort, Stupak appeared on national television talk shows, touting his various promotions. But he topped himself in 1991 by announcing that he would build the world's largest tower, in the "space needle" style, on the Vegas World property. Convinced by the Federal Aviation Administration to cut its height by a few stories, Stupak proceeded with construction. In 1993, the pod atop the emerging tower spectacularly caught fire, showering burning debris on spectators below and forcing the temporary evacuation of the casino. Two years later little Vegas World closed as a mammoth helicopter lifted the final pieces of the landmark tower resort—dubbed the Stratosphere—into place. The $550-million observation deck, revolving restaurant, hotel, casino, roller coaster, and wedding chapel in the sky—made possible by Stupak's bravado and a healthy contribution from financial investors—opened in 1996. Stupak was lucky to make the debut. He had crashed his motorcycle several months earlier and spent five weeks in a coma. Entirely too flamboyant, even for glittery Las Vegas, Stupak was eventually eased out of the Stratosphere operation. In *No Limit*, John L. Smith's unauthorized 1997 biography,

Elvis Presley was serving in the Army in Germany when he met fourteen-year-old Priscilla Beaulieu. They eventually wed on May 1, 1967 at the Aladdin Hotel. Now "Elvis chapels" and weddings are Las Vegas staples.

Stupak is described as "one of the city's neon dinosaurs—perhaps the last of the carnival-style operators that once proliferated around town."

Steve Wynn was a Philadelphia business-school graduate who moved to Las Vegas in 1967, buying a piece of the New Frontier Hotel. He earned his reputation for shrewd dealing by purchasing a sliver of land next to Caesars Palace—owned by Howard Hughes and used by Caesars as a parking lot—immediately selling it to Caesars for $2.25 million, and then using the profits, plus those from the sale of his share in the New Frontier, to buy the historic Golden Nugget downtown. Wynn transformed it from a fading icon into a classy resort hotel. With profits from an Atlantic City casino investment, he bought the old Castaways, closed it, and in 1989 assembled the stylish, South Seas-themed Mirage—the first new Las Vegas resort in sixteen years. Then, on nearly vacant land next door, his Mirage Resorts group erected Treasure Island, aimed at a more modest clientele. But in 1998 Wynn again targeted the elite with the addition of the upscale Bellagio on the site of the old Dunes, whose implosion Wynn signaled by firing a cannon from Treasure Island, half a mile down the Strip. Where Las Vegas had been a slightly tacky oasis for gamblers and family vacationers, Wynn's ventures confirmed the obvious: Vegas was evolving into a destination for high rollers, *haute monde* shoppers, and

Milton Prell's Aladdin Hotel, named for the owner of a magic lamp in "Arabian Nights" legend, opened in 1966. Grown dowdy, the Aladdin was imploded in 1998 to make room for a superresort of the same name.

jet setters from around the world. Outside all three of his new megaresorts, however, Wynn made sure the masses were entertained with ostentatious shows: an exploding volcano at Mirage, a pirate battle at Treasure Island, and graceful fountain choreography at Bellagio. In March 2000, Mirage Resorts sold out to Kirk Kerkorian's MGM group for a tidy $4.4 billion—in cash. Steve Wynn's reported share approached $500 million.

Las Vegas may be a fantasyland, but it's not Shangri-La for everyone. In a city where a carhop can take home $50,000 a year and tell Internal Revenue about only part of it, it's hard to convince students to stay in school. "The locals refer to this as 'the golden handcuffs,'" Paul Swift, a philosophy professor at Rhode Island College in Providence, wrote in the Las Vegas *Chronicle-Review*. "People can live in prosperity, but they can barely ever leave." Swift added that, when he was a student at the University of Nevada at Las Vegas, he wanted to take a course in classical Greek. None was offered, but there was a college-level course in "sportsbook management," helping people become bookies. In a city where a free drink is as close as the nearest blackjack table, alcoholism is a persistent presence, and compulsive-gambling addiction is rampant. "Despite the countless personal bankruptcies, the ruined marriages, the suicides that have occurred in the state since Nevada legalized gambling in 1931, the Legislature had never scheduled a public hearing to discuss the [gambling-addiction] issue," the *Review-Journal* wrote on March 16, 2001. That is, until that very day. Witnesses pointed out that while some other states had spent millions of dollars for treatment and education programs, the extent of Nevada's response was to require casinos and other settings with slots and table games to post the toll-free number for the problem-gamblers' hotline.

Eccentric Hollywood producer, daredevil aviator, and secretive entrepreneur Howard Hughes (below) took over the penthouse floor of the Desert Inn in 1966. Asked to leave, he bought the place—and several other Vegas casinos.

The American West, where recorded history is sometimes less than two centuries old and preservation societies are just now gaining enough clout to preserve historic structures, has always been about growth and boomtowns. But even in garish Las Vegas, growth has also enhanced civic life in the form of new parks, better schools, affordable housing, and plenty of jobs. No longer a "low-culture" wasteland, Sin City can now trumpet its ballet, philharmonic and chamber orchestras, one of the nation's newest and more ambitious universities, and amazing visual artists who produce not only incredible neon art but also remarkable street sculptures.

But never forget the foundation upon which this is built: Without gambling and risqué revues that turn visitors into voyeurs, there would be no bustling economy to underwrite the arts. Las Vegas has turned a touch narcissistic in its tourist fairylands, but any old Joe can still drop a quarter in a slot machine at the 7-Eleven, the airport, grocery and liquor stores, and myriad other places in town.

Built with gritty determination in forbidding terrain, nurtured by plucky rapscallions, reinvented over and over again by entrepreneurs who bet fortunes on the city's future and won, Las Vegas has exploded into America's desert spectacle. Anyone who has traced its evolution from a dusty watering hole into a world entertainment destination would be wise not to underestimate Las Vegas's potential for unimagined reinventions yet to come.

In the 1990s the sleepy South Strip exploded into a procession of hotel-casino palaces with the opening of Excalibur, the Luxor, and the Mandalay Bay (overleaf).

In 1999 the $950-million, thirty-seven-hundred-room Mandalay Bay (right)—the flagship property of the Mandalay Resort Group that also owns the Excalibur, Luxor, and Circus Circus—opened on the site of the old Hacienda Hotel. The gleaming-gold hotel features the ninety-thousand-square-foot Shark Reef aquarium; a twelve-thousand-seat auditorium that has accommodated concerts, touring Broadway shows, and championship prize fights; and an eleven-acre, manmade lake (above) on which six-foot waves can be created. Part of the resort is devoted to a hotel-within-a-hotel: the exclusive Four Seasons. The Mandalay Bay has a shopping gallery, a thirty-thousand-square-foot spa, and thirteen restaurants, from a noodle shop to an expansive seafood buffet. In the tradition of many Strip resorts that feature their own wedding chapels, betrothed guests need not even leave the property.

The Luxor (opposite and above), designed by Las Vegas architect Veldon Simpson, opened in 1993. Its stunning onyx-tinted glass pyramid—a life-size replica of the Temple of Ramses II that is regularly washed by a remarkable moving "squeegee"—was joined by two zig-zag-shaped towers three years later. The building's xenon light, slicing into space, has become a Vegas landmark. This billion-candle-power engineering marvel is forty times as powerful as a strong searchlight. Ancient Egyptian symbolism continues in the Sphinx entryway, a barge course around the "River Nile," and visualizations of Cleopatra and King Tut, including a life-size replica of the latter's tomb. Pyramid guests experience the world's largest atrium (overleaf) at twenty-nine million square feet. They reach their rooms on "inclinators" traveling up thirty stories at a 39° angle. The Luxor is a dreamland for hiero-glyphics scholars; the hotel is replete with authentic copies.

With its gaudy, illu-
minated cluster of
turreted towers,
Excalibur (opposite
and above), which
lowered its draw-
bridge in 1990,
appears to be a cross
between a medieval

fortress and a fanciful
toyland. Excalibur
was the magical sword
that Arthur of
Camelot succeeded
in pulling from a
block of stone. Bor-
rowing from the older
Circus Circus, another

Mandalay Resort
Group family-
oriented property,
Excalibur's "World
of King Arthur"
also caters to young,
old, and people in
between. The hotel
stages a show in which

a fifty-one-foot, fire-
breathing dragon is
banished by the
sorcerer Merlin. Else-
where, the hotel is the
morning-till-night
stage for court jesters,
strolling troubadours,
and even a joust over

dinner. Its shops
are the only place
in Las Vegas where
one can buy a suit—
of armor. Directly
across the street at the
Tropicana is an
arcade of a different
sort (overleaf).

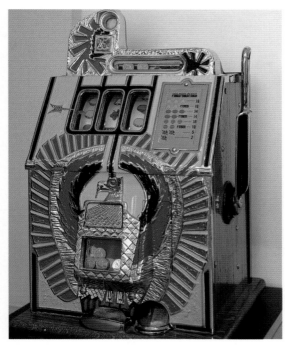

Investors gambled
when they opened the
Tropicana in 1957 a
mile out the desert
highway that would
become the famous
"Strip." But nobody
could miss the Tropi-
cana's stunning neon
sign, shaped like a
gushing fountain.
Inside the "Tiffany of
the Strip," long
famous for its Folies
Bergere revue,
visitors still gawk at
the leaded-glass
casino ceiling (left).

The Casino Legends
Hall of Fame at the
Tropicana displays
twenty thousand
classic Vegas items,
including pho-
tographs, costumes,
and vintage mechan-
ical slot machines
(above). If, as it's
sometimes said,
Las Vegas is a façade,
one of the most
amazing examples is
the compressed Man-
hattan skyline at the
New York New York
resort (overleaf).

If your imagination runs wild, you can believe you're viewing the real Big Apple and not the outdoor set that is the New York New York Hotel and Casino (left), which opened in 1997 across from the MGM Grand where two tired motels and a gas station had stood. The tallest structure in the $460-million complex is the "Empire State Building" at 529 feet, about half the real structure's height. Providentially, no "World Trade Center" twin towers were included. The "Manhattan Express" roller coaster weaves past icons like "the Brooklyn Bridge" (above). Inside, guest rooms are creatively distributed among the towers, and the gaming space evokes a Central Park theme.

39

The $1-billion MGM
Grand Hotel, Casino,
and Theme Park
(opposite and domi-
nating the mid-strip
landscape, left), which
opened in 1993, is
grand, all right. With
more than five
thousand rooms, it is
the world's largest
hotel. The resort's
trademark lion is the
Western Hemisphere's
largest bronze sculp-
ture. Snell Johnson's
creation includes
more than 1,660
welded pieces and
weighs one hundred
thousand pounds.
The original MGM
Grand, up the Strip
at what is now the
Bally's site, was the
scene of a 1980 fire
in which eighty-four
people died. At the
Monte Carlo across
the street, master
magician, illusionist,
and escape artist
Lance Burton
(overleaf) has been
a fixture for many
years. Unlike
most Vegas perform-
ers, Burton takes
special pains to
invite children from
the audience to
participate in his
extravaganzas.

The Holiday Inn's Boardwalk Hotel and Casino (opposite and above), which opened in 1968, affects a jaunty amusement park theme. Whereas earlier Strip properties emphasized their entertainment lounges, swimming pools, and drive-up rooms; and later mega-resorts constructed elaborate mythic environments set well back from the street; the Boardwalk flaunts a come-on-in approach—complete with hurdy-gurdy music—right on the sidewalk. The 654-room hotel keeps a niche amid the surrounding megaresorts by emphasizing its central location, affordable rooms and cafés, low minimums at the gaming tables, and friendly staff. The Boardwalk features Vegas's only twenty-four-hour buffet. Holiday Inn completed a wholesale facelift and construction of an additional hotel tower in 1996. The $785- million, 2,916-room Paris Las Vegas Casino Resort (overleaf) opened in 1999 between Bally's and the Aladdin. Paris Las Vegas is modeled after the fabled Hotel de Ville in the French capital.

A fifty-story, half-scale replica of the Eiffel Tower—complete with an elegant French restaurant eleven stories above ground—is but one Parisian-style icon at the Paris Las Vegas (opposite).

Others include a faux Arc de Triomphe, Paris Opera House, and Louvre. The resort's casino features a ceiling painted to resemble the Parisian sky at twilight. Gaming entrepreneur

Steve Wynn's $1.6-billion Tuscan-inspired Bellagio (above), named after a town on Italy's Lake Como, opened a year later across the street where the former Dunes resort, with its trade-

mark thirty-five-foot-high lighted sultan, once stood. The Bellagio's conservatory, art gallery, and Rodeo Drive-caliber shops accent its luxury appeal. Outside on an eight-acre lake every

fifteen minutes to half-hour, more than one thousand fountains produce swirling water shows (overleaf) with themes like "the Oarsmen," bathed in lights and set to classi-cal or show music.

The grandiose buildings on the Las Vegas Strip (opposite) are the work of what Deanna DeMatteo, creator of the most comprehensive website on the Las Vegas Strip's history, calls "dreamweavers."

Whereas their magic first spread from downtown southward along once-desolate Las Vegas Boulevard, futurists predict that another concentration of yet-to-be-imagined attractions is inevitable some-

where else, off today's beaten track in this tourist and convention destination. In 1993 Bally's (above) opened on a prime site at the intersection of the Strip and Flamingo Road on the site of the little

1967-vintage Bonanza Motel and massive, original MGM Grand. The latter, tragically remembered for its catastrophic fire in 1980, had been the world's largest hotel but had fallen to

fifteenth place with the opening of monster properties elsewhere on the Strip. Designer Brad Friedmutter's glowing people mover and porte-cochère (overleaf) became Bally's signature.

When Caesars Palace, financed in part with a $10.6-million loan from a Teamsters Union pension fund, opened in 1966 (opposite), it upped the ante among Las Vegas resorts. Until then, only modest proper- ties, better known for their lounge acts than their accommodations, were situated on the Strip. The hottest gaming action was still downtown. Caesars was the brainchild of Jay Sarno, who owned a series of cabana- style motels across the country. He and architect Melvin Grossman designed a decadent Roman entertainment spa where gamblers and ordinary tourists alike could be pampered. Caesars infused the Roman décor into every aspect of its eye- popping complex, from the cypress-lined entryway and court of fountains to the trendy Forum shop. Statuary was everywhere. Through several reno- vations, Caesars has more than quadrupled in size. Its Magical Empire (above), in a catacomb far below the resort, combines magic and meals. "Wizards" entertain diners with comedy and sleight- of-hand before a full- scale magic show.

An enduring highlight of a Caesars stay is a splash in one of three elegant and enormous pools (left) in the "Garden of the Gods." Pools were always an attraction in Las Vegas, especially in the blistering summertime, but these outdid them all. Even by Las Vegas standards, the announcement that Canadian superstar Celine Dion (above) had signed to perform at Caesars, two hundred nights a year for three years beginning in 2003 in a new four-thousand-seat amphitheater—modeled after Rome's Colosseum and built specifically for this engagement—was a blockbuster. Her show, designed to include more then seventy other performers as well and combining the elements of a live show and a music video, was designed by the Cirque du Soleil review creators.

Caesars Palace black-jack dealer "Grave-yard Jim" Ross opposite) is a Las Vegas legend. He gets his nickname from his preference for the overnight shift when, like many night-owl dealers, he has a loyal following. Keeping track of chip values, bets, and payouts becomes second nature to a skilled dealer. Inter-personal aplomb is rarer. The flashy Flamingo Hotel (above), boasts a fifteen-acre, Caribbean-style "water playground." Fittingly, a flock of Chilean flamingos is one feature of the resort's wildlife habitat. Penguins, turtles, swans, ducks, Guinea fowl, parrots, pheasants, turtles, and about one thousand Koi and goldfish are also part of the menagerie. The resort—the third and most spec-tacular built on the emerging Strip— once included elabo-rate escape tunnels for its mobster owner, "Bugsy" Siegel. Today the Flamingo makes light of its nefarious beginning: one of its auditoriums is even called "Bugsy's Celebrity Theatre."

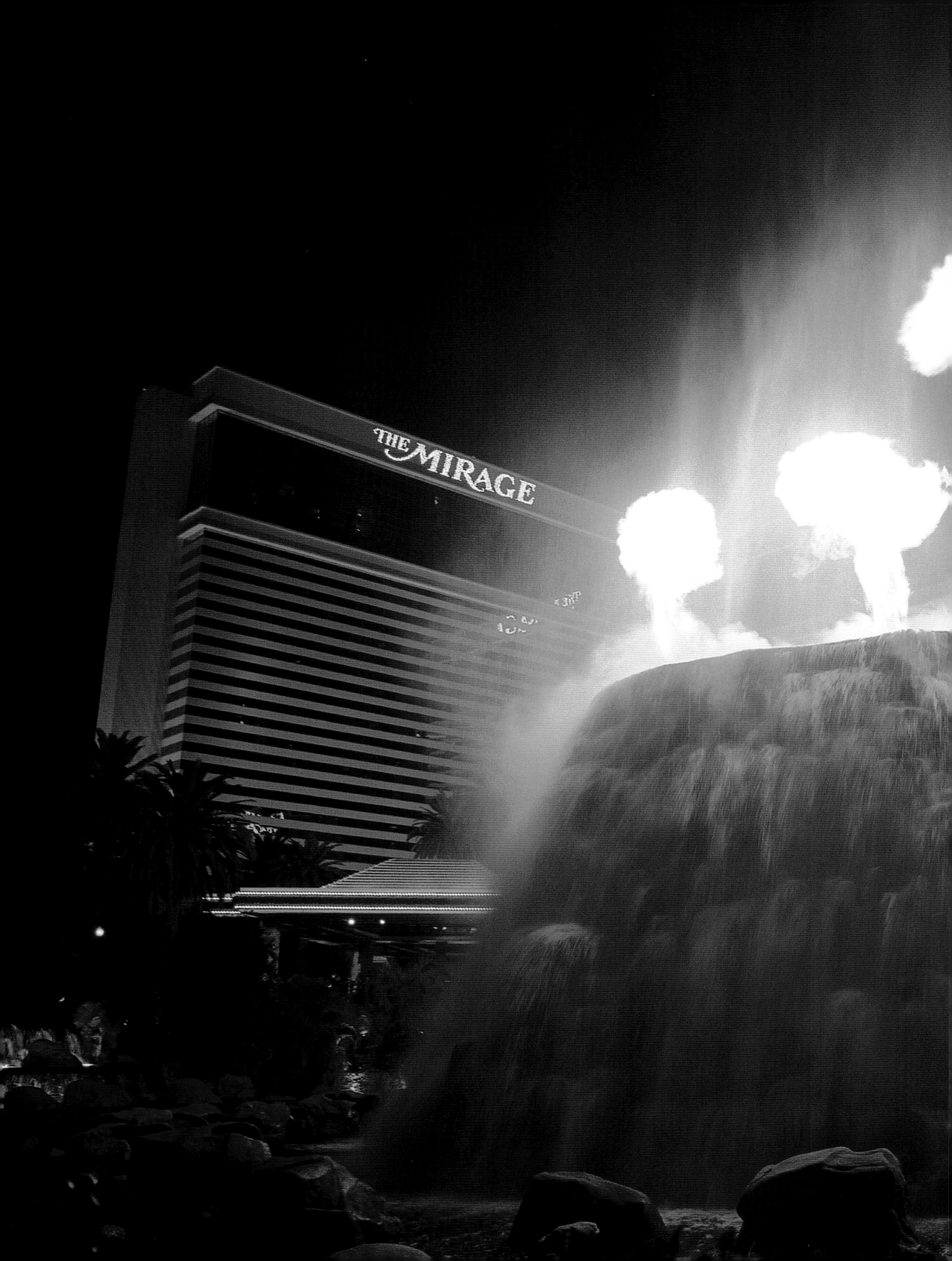
THE MIRAGE

All of Las Vegas can seem like a mirage, but the resort casino of that name did not appear until 1989. Its one-hundred-foot exploding volcano (left), dolphin and white-tiger habitat, trendy shops, and megashow starring Siegfried and Roy accentuated Vegas's turnaround from a gamblers' retreat to an international tourist destination. Mirage Resorts' chairman Steve Wynn turned away from in-your-face light displays to a refined environment in which every family member would feel comfortable. Across the street, similarly themed River Boat and Holiday casinos sprouted where a couple of meager motels, the Tumbleweed and the Pyramids had stood. They later combined under the Harrah's Casinos umbrella into a single entity with a Mardi Gras theme. Harrah's jesters (above) replaced steamboat wheels and smokestacks as mid-Strip icons.

In 2003, Siegfried and Roy's legions of fans were horrified by the unexpected and nearly fatal onstage attack of Roy Horn by one of his most-trusted white tigers. The sudden mauling of this gentle animal-lover halted one of Las Vegas's most-popular spectacles at the Mirage. The lavish productions (right) of these German-born "masters of the impossible" combined inconceivable illusions, human and mechanical choreography, sensuous costumes and lighting, and animal magnetism. Siegfried (on the right, above) handled most of the magic and audience patter, while Roy was the foil for dangerous stunts and tricks. Just how dangerous, a stunned audience would discover that shocking night. Siegfried and Roy's "secret garden" of more than forty endangered species still remains open next to the resort.

The Mirage makes one of its opulent villas, otherwise reserved for very high rollers, available to superstar Paul Anka (left), an enduring headliner at top Vegas clubs. Former child prodigy, teen idol, and writer of more than nine hundred songs—including "My Way"—Anka has recorded more than 125 albums. "Las Vegas fine dining" is no longer an oxymoron. Superb restaurants include the Mirage's five-star Renoir's (opposite). It is ringed by original paintings, including four by Pierre-Auguste Renoir. Shown is the 1880 "The Garden of Essai in Algiers." Next door, several times nightly outside the 2,900-room Treasure Island Hotel and Casino, passersby press for the best view of the pyrotechnic clash (overleaf) between "H. M. S. Brittannia" and the pirate ship "Hispaniola" in the "Sea Battle at Buccaneer Bay."

Gondoliers paddle past Grand Canal shops at the $1.5-billion Venetian (opposite), which opened in 1999. This resort casino touts its average room size—seven hundred square feet—and its five-acre pool deck. Many of its boutiques were newly introduced to the United States. Adding to the Venetian's cachet is the Guggenheim Las Vegas Museum (above), comprised of several galleries. The museum is designed to accommodate several special exhibitions at once. The underside of the museum's skylight presents a facsimile of the central scene from Michelangelo's Sistine Chapel ceiling. The long-running inaugural exhibit at one of the Guggenheim galleries was a perfect Las Vegas fit; it featured "The Art of the Motorcycle." Although the Guggenheim in New York concentrates on modern and contemporary art, the Las Vegas gallery includes a joint venture with the State Hermitage Museum in St. Petersburg, Russia, in which masterpieces are showcased.

Celebrities cloned at Madame Tussaud's Wax Museum inside the Venetian include Marilyn Monroe and Judy Garland (opposite). No velvet ropes keep fans from these figures. Cus-tomers are invited to touch them and appre-ciate the work that Tussaud's says is "accurate down to the tiniest detail, including every hair, eyelash, and dimple." The work on Benjamin "Bugsy" Siegel's figure (above) was done from pho-tographs. The Brooklyn-born Mob killer, Hollywood playboy, and Las Vegas extortionist and racing-wire owner who built the Flamingo Hotel in fits and starts, has been dead since 1947. He was gunned down in Los Angeles— allegedly for skimming money from Flamingo investors. One of the first celebrity gangsters since Al Capone, Ben Siegel—he detested "Bugsy," which was given him for his tendency to "go bugs" when rankled—lived to see the Flamingo open the day after Christmas, 1946, but not much longer.

Madame Tussaud's Wax Museum artisans recreate the faces of their figures from precise measurements taken during personal sittings or studies of archival materials. One apropos subject is Vegas legend Frank Sinatra (opposite). He played to celebrity crowds at the Sands, then painted the town with his Rat Pack drinking buddies. Sinatra later switched to other Vegas resorts after a falling out with Sands management. The view from the mid-Strip looking north (left) shows the contrast between the megaresorts that sprouted along Las Vegas Boulevard and the intimate downtown casinos beyond the Stratosphere tower. In 2002 the Las Vegas Monorail Company announced it would extend its driverless monorail northward from its two existing stops to Sahara Avenue, with plans to eventually expand all the way to the Fremont Street Experience.

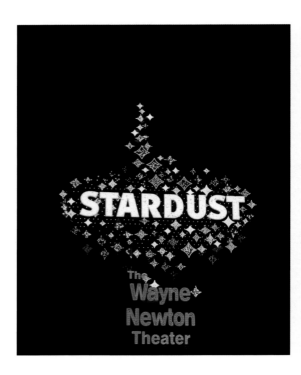

Wayne Newton (right) earned Las Vegas's richest contract in 1999 when he signed at the Stardust for $25 million a year. "The Midnight Idol" had first played Vegas at age fifteen forty years earlier. He owned the Aladdin Casino for a time, declared bankruptcy, but recovered as the heartthrob of visiting housewives. The Stardust opened in 1958 as a resort for the proletariat. It turned the old Royal Nevada on the property into a convention center. Famous for its Le Lido De Paris spectaculars, which ran for thirty-one years after deviating from Vegas's lounge-star fixation, the resort introduced its 188-foot-tall signature sign (above) that sprinkles neon and incandescent stardust.

The Guardian Angel Cathedral (opposite), located across from the Stardust, one-half block off the Las Vegas Strip on land donated by casino owners, serves the Roman Catholic Diocese of Las Vegas. More than 75 percent of those who attend Mass on any given Sunday are tourists. The cathedral, built in 1963, seats eleven hundred. It is managed by Viatorians—clerics of St. Viator of the Chicago Province—with headquarters in suburban Chicago. The building is replete with artwork, including mosaics, murals, and stained-glass windows. One (left), by Isabel Piczek, mixes Christian themes with depictions of quite secular Las Vegas sites. Other real-world touches: The cathedral has a gift shop, and the back page of the church bulletin is filled with advertising from local businesses— including a casino.

The La Concha Motel (above), whose conch-shell design seemed so futuristic in 1961, made it into the new millennium—still advertising color TV as an amenity—as one of the last low-rise properties amid monster resorts in the heart of the Strip. "When you've been here a long time and you don't have a big mortgage, it's not very hard to survive," owner Fred Doumani told the Las Vegas Review-Journal. *The article quoted guests as appreciating the small scale, relative privacy, and parking where they could keep an eye on their auto-mobiles. The nearby Riviera features the Crazy Girls show-girls—seen welcoming visitors at the famous, retro "Fabulous Las Vegas" sign down at the other end of the Strip (opposite). In performance, the girls' costumes are consid-erably skimpier. The sign, erected in the late 1950s, has moved several times as development marched southward.*

Liberace starred at the lavish opening of the Riviera (opposite) as the city's first high-rise resort—just nine stories. A 1990 facelift created its phantasmal neon façade. In the Riviera's colorful history, Liberace got $50,000 a week to headline at the Clover Showroom—later called the Versailles Theatre. The Rivera's second operator, Gus Greenbaum, and his wife were rubbed out in a presumed Mob hit; and the property twice went bankrupt. But it survived and thrived, in part by showcasing several lavish productions. Among them is the "Evening With La Cage" revue first introduced in 1985. It's a sensual romp starring big-name celebrities. Well, not exactly. The La Cage "girls," plus Michael Jackson (above), are dead-ringer impersonators whose star among stars is Frank Marino as Joan Rivers. Out front of the Riviera is a life-sized bronze cast of the cast's, uh, posteriors.

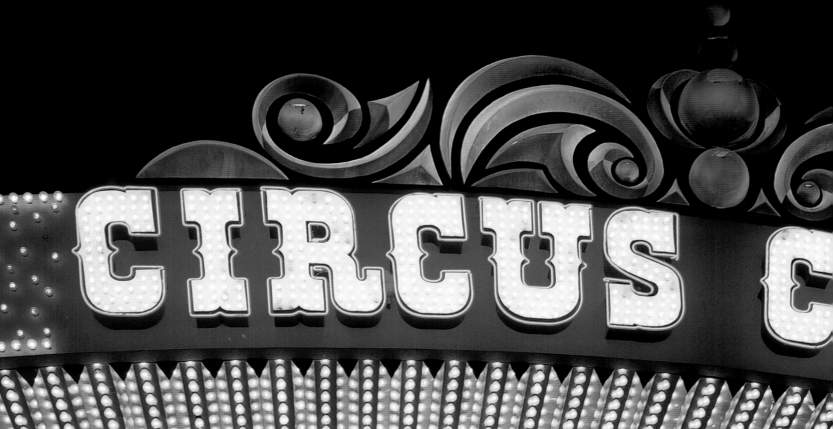

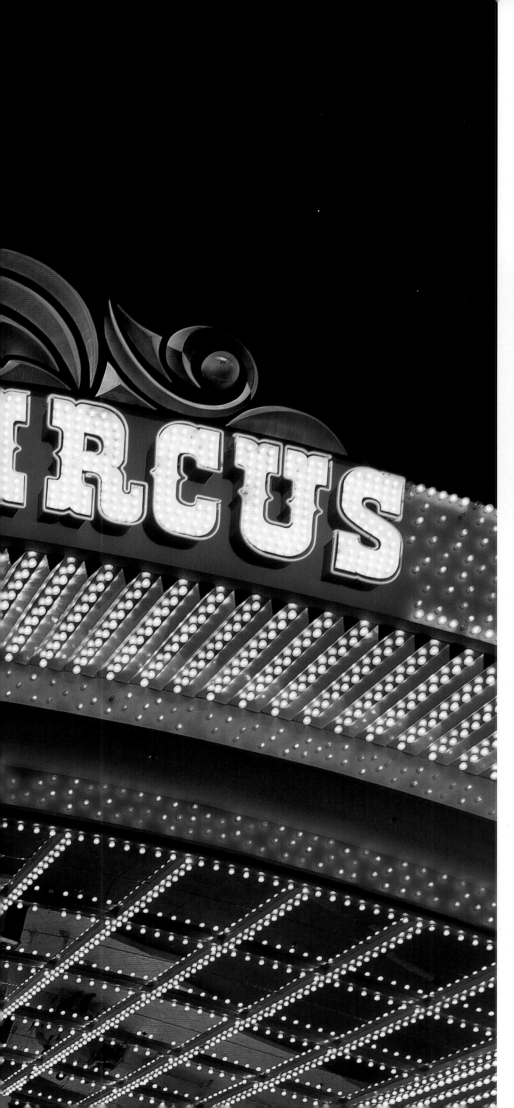

In 1968 Circus Circus (left) opened on a grand scale as a family-oriented companion to Caesars Palace. Inside its pink and white circus tent-shaped "big top" was an oval casino the size of a football field. Aerialists, clowns, and acrobats cavorted, a "midway" offered carnival games and concessions, and slot machines played music. In 1993 Circus Circus exaggerated scale again when it opened the Adventure-dome, America's largest indoor amusement park. The Sahara (above) replaced the old Club Bingo in 1952 on a Strip location once so empty that airplanes landed there. A 1999 renovation produced the NASCAR Café, complete with videos of stock-car races, NASCAR merchandise, and the world's largest car—at three tons—displayed above the bar. And the Sahara's SPEED roller-coaster is Vegas's fastest.

Las Vegas's $550-million Stratosphere Hotel Casino and Tower (opposite and seen looking north toward downtown, right) opened in 1996. It was the brainchild of Bob Stupak, who owned a modest casino, Vegas World, on the site at the top of the Strip on the edge of downtown. At 1,149 feet high, the Stratosphere is the tallest structure west of the Mississippi River. It boasts the world's two highest thrill rides. One rockets riders 160 feet into the air in 2.5 seconds at four Gs' force. The other circles the outer edge of the tower, 112 stories up, making six clockwise rotations and banking at thirty-two-degree angles. The observation desk and revolving restaurant on the twelve-story upper "pod" provide spectacular views of the valley, distant mountains, and Vegas Strip.

In the mid-1990s, the City of Las Vegas responded to the precipitous decline in tourist traffic downtown brought on by the area's decline and the explosion of enticing megaresorts on the Las Vegas Strip outside city limits in Clark County. The burghers accepted architect Jon Jerde's audacious concept of turning five city blocks into a pedestrian and entertainment mall, with four surmounted by a canopy of two million lights. Now, each nighttime hour until midnight, streetlights and casino signs dim, and one of seven fully animated sound and light shows (opposite and above), dubbed the "Fremont Street Experience," unfolds overhead. The choreographed lights and 218 giant speakers directed by thirty-six computers produce everything from snorting steers to rock shows. The clean, safe, and effervescent environment has been good for properties like the Fremont Hotel and Casino (overleaf) that line downtown's old casino row.

The old Hacienda Hotel's neon horse and rider (above), installed in 1967 on the far South Strip, was rescued after being discarded. Remounted downtown where Las Vegas Boulevard meets the Fremont Street Experience, it was the first vintage sign to be reinstalled by the new Neon Museum. The city's most beloved outdoor icon is forty-foot-tall "Vegas Vic" (right), who showed off his famous smoldering cigarette, neon wink, waving arm, and a voice that boomed, "Howdy, pardner" above the now-defunct Pioneer Club. Vic, too, is part of Fremont Street's rejuvenated "Glitter Gulch." Undulating signs enticed visitors heading out Boulder Highway to Hoover Dam to stay in motels (opposite) that are now showing their years.

VALLEY MOTEL
AIR CONDITIONED

NO VACANCY

WELCOME
SEE OUR NICE ROOMS

Almost literally within the shadow of the glittering Strip, a stone's throw from the MGM Grand, the Tropicana Motor Park (above) is a vestige of Las Vegas's hardscrabble days.

Such parks are fast disappearing, but others can still be found near Nellis Air Force Base. They were a prominent part of the landscape when Vegas was a more transient town, and dealers, pit bosses, and showgirls came and went. Brides and grooms still do, since Las Vegas is the world's wedding capital. Each year more than one-hundred thousand people tie the knot in Vegas, which requires neither blood tests nor a nuptial waiting period. Founded in 1940, the Wee Kirk o'the Heather (opposite) is the longest-running among dozens of marriage chapels. Among its "packages" is an "Elvis Wedding," in which an Elvis impersonator walks the bride down the aisle and croons three love songs.

Wee kirk o' the Heather
WEDDING
CHAPEL
MARRIAGE INFORMATION
EVERYTHING ARRANGED
INCLUDING LICENSE
GOWNS TUXEDOS

Drive Thru
Lover's Lane
Weddings

Drive Thru
Lover's Lane
Weddings

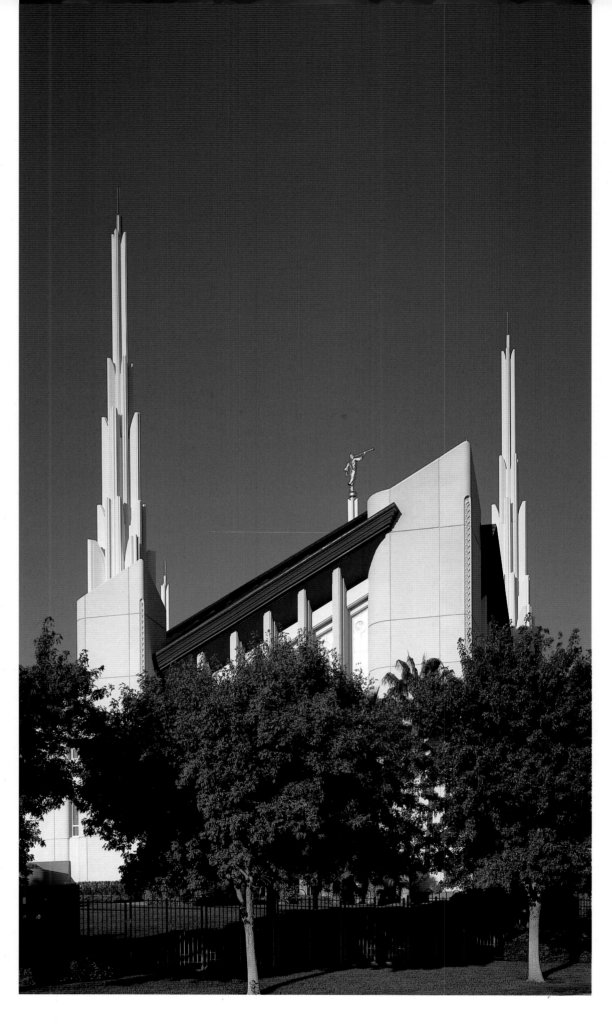

Not all striking architectural statements in Las Vegas involve neon and light displays. The Lied Discovery Children's Museum downtown (opposite) and Mormon Temple (left) east of town take advantage of the valley's ample sun to accentuate their sharp lines and shadows. The nonprofit Lied Museum, which is routinely voted the city's best cultural attraction, opened in 1990. It packs more than one hundred hands-on exhibits into twenty-five-thousand square feet. The $18-million, granite Mormon Temple, dedicated at the foot of Frenchman Mountain in 1989, has six spires, the largest of which, topped by a gold-leafed statue of the Angel Moroni, rises 119 feet. At night the structure is bathed in white light. Las Vegas, founded by Mormon missionaries, still has a significant membership in the Church of Jesus Christ of Latter-Day Saints.

Neon, thought by some to have become passé in shimmering Las Vegas, made a stunning comeback in two of the city's newest properties, the Palms (above) and the Rio (opposite), west of the Strip. The Rio All-Suites Hotel and Casino, which opened in 1990 and quickly expanded seven times, takes an elegant, uncomplicated approach to cladding itself in neon. It was built by Anthony Marnell, designer of many imposing Strip resorts, including the Mirage and Treasure Island, which together supplanted the old Dunes resort. Because it is centrally located but removed from the Las Vegas Strip, Vegas's first "boutique hotel," the $265-million Palms (above), which opened in 2001, offers a unique view of the length and breadth of the Strip off to the east. Casino resort signs of a much less sophisticated sort, and different era, can be found in the city's "boneyard" (overleaf).

In a dusty downtown lot, bygone Las Vegas signs that went to scrap are forming the foundation for the city's Neon Museum Boneyard and Visitors Center. Other signs were mothballed by Young Electric Sign Co., a pioneer sign designer and builder. YESCO is steadily donating signs from its own boneyard to the city for the Neon Museum. Many of the creations, such as the billiards player (left) from old west-side Pocket Lounge, employed no neon at all. But they are iconic sculptures, representative of the brash promotional mindset of this unabashed town. The Golden Nugget sign (above) came from the 1946 landmark Glitter Gulch casino whose name fits one of its prominent displays: a sixty-one-pound gold nugget, largest in the world on public view.

Treasures in the Neon Museum's sign boneyard include the silver slipper (above) from the Strip casino of the same name, and a magic lamp (right) from the early Aladdin. The Silver Slipper opened in 1950 as a gambling hall, chuckwagon buffet, and burlesque venue within the Last Frontier Village theme park. The slipper rotated atop the casino. In 1988 the Silver Slipper was demolished for a parking lot. On Fremont Street, the Neon Museum remounted a different, lighted Aladdin's Lamp that had perched atop the old hotel's fifteen-story highway sign. City cultural officials receive many requests from nostalgia buffs to see these reminders of places they may have stayed or gambled. The Neon Museum's "adopt-a-sign" campaign raises money to refurbish historic signs and remount some on city streets.

Las Vegas's Chinatown is centered in Chinatown Plaza, a mélange of Asian restaurants, art and jewelry shops, and even a dinosaur exhibit west of the Strip on Spring Mountain Road.

Notable at this strip shopping center is a statue (opposite) depicting a Chinese fable about a monkey and a monk. Classic "road art" is fast disappearing from Las Vegas, but one

remaining example is the pink elephant at the Diamond Inn (above), an older motor court-style motel hanging on amid the building boom on the South Strip. The world's

largest private collection of Elvis Presley memorabilia—including some of his cars, jewelry, furniture, stage costumes like an outrageous gold lamé outfit, military uniforms, and a pair of his

famous blue-suede shoes—is displayed at the Elvis-A-Rama Museum (overleaf), a favorite Las Vegas tour-bus stop. The King's music fills the showroom, just west of the New Frontier.

Glitz, kitsch, a bigger-than-life aura. This describes not just Las Vegas but also one of its outrageous per-formers—Liberace, born Wladziu Valentino Liberace in West Allis, Wisconsin. Classically trained on the grand piano, he performed with the Chicago Symphony and gradually added extravagant trade-marks to his reper-toire: the candelabra, the bejeweled jackets, and the flourishing keyboard style. A star on television, at Carnegie Hall, and on record, he became Las Vegas's highest-paid performer. "Mr. Showmanship's" legend is preserved at the nonprofit Liberace Museum east of the Strip. Among his arti-facts on display: the world's largest rhine-stone; eighteen rare pianos, including a rhinestone-covered Baldwin (above); and some of his ornate Rolls Royces (left).

The Clark County Museum on Boulder Highway in Henderson includes a heritage section (above) featuring the Tuscarora Jail from the 1880s and, to the right, remnants of an Old West town that was constructed on the Las Vegas Strip in the 1950s. The most eclectic house in electric Las Vegas is "Lonnie's Castle" (opposite), the home of accordion-playing neurosurgeon and longtime Nevada lieutenant governor, Lonnie Hammargren. Built in 1969 as a standard four-bedroom frame stucco dwelling, the house, formally called Castillo del Sol, overflows with an eccentric's delights, including a Mayan pyramid, a planetarium, one of Liberace's honky-tonk pianos, motorcycles belonging to movie stars like Steve McQueen, and a bathroom ringed by Native American pictographs. Among the attractions outside: a locomotive from the Yucca nuclear test site, a model of Hoover Dam, and—in a pool—a functioning submarine from the movie "Sea Hunt."

Just seven miles from the Las Vegas Strip, Henderson, the nation's fastest-growing city from the mid-1990s into the twenty-first century, replaced Reno as Nevada's second-largest city. It is a golfers' paradise and the locus of several master-planned communities. In Henderson's Green Valley section, two painted bronze golfers (right) "compare notes" outside the Legacy Golf Club. Real players practice their putting at Reflection Bay Golf Club (opposite), whose 7,261-yard course was designed by Jack Nicklaus near the manmade, 320-acre Lake Las Vegas. The sprawling Hyatt resort, spa, and European-style casino looms along the lake (overleaf). "Executive homes" and Mediterranean-style villas, a yacht club, and private beaches dot the hillsides of this "guard-gated" community. Other Vegas planned "golf suburbs" like Summerlin have also helped turn forsaken desert into verdant oases of refined living.

Pleasant homes line historic Boulder City (above), built in the 1930s for workers constructing Boulder Dam—later renamed for the incumbent president Herbert Hoover. The little model city, which remained a government town for almost thirty years, was—and still is—a Nevada aberration: gambling and alcohol sales are prohibited. The sixty-story-high Hoover Dam (right)—more massive than the largest Egyptian pyramid—tamed the raging Colorado River by bottling up Black Canyon on the Nevada-Arizona border. Laborers working in blistering heat fashioned the 6,600,000-ton behemoth by pouring one-hundred-sixty thousand cubic yards of concrete a month for two years. The reservoir that rose behind the dam became Lake Mead (overleaf), now a national recreation area that stretches to the lower reaches of the Grand Canyon.

Although the desert immediately surrounding Las Vegas is desolate and uninviting, just twenty miles west of town the terrain turns spectacular in the Red Rock National Conservation Area (left and above). This land was under a deep sea for five hundred million years, during which marine life left skeletons that piled up in what is now limestone layers as much as nine thousand feet thick. Evaporation of the giant sea into a Sahara-like desert etched stunning formations, three thousand feet high. Colors range from white to orange to a deep red, the latter resulting from the weathering of iron particles. The recreation area's canyons are a favorite destination for rock-climbing and for hiking, biking, picnicking, and photo-taking along a thirteen-mile loop road.

Driving south out of Las Vegas toward California is like opening a time capsule. The desert terrain (above) is not much different from the old landscape where the Vegas Strip sits today. Little stone cabins (right) were built by hand in the 1920s near tiny Sloan, Nevada, along the two-lane Vegas-to-Los Angeles highway, parts of which still parallel Interstate 15. The adjacent roadhouse café served "pop" and beer to thirsty travelers beginning in the 1950s. When you approach dusty crossroad towns like Jean and Primm near the California line, you get one last chance to legally hit blackjack at quaint casinos. The three-hundred-room Nevada Landing in Jean (overleaf) opened in 1989.

Index

Page numbers in italics refer to illustrations.

Aladdin, 10, 11, 13–15, *19, 20, 45, 104*
Anka, Paul, *67*

Bally's and (original) MGM Grand, 10, 11, 17–18, *41, 45, 53*

Las Vegas began around springs that rose from aquifers in the blistering Mojave desert. Remnants remain at the Old Las Vegas Mormon Fort State Historic Park, where, in 1855, thirty men, sent from Utah by Brigham Young, founded a mission. The missionaries and Paiute people congregated around the only grass for miles in "Las Vegas," Spanish for "The Meadows."

Bellagio, 9, 11, 12, 18, 20, 21, *49*
Bennett, William, 18–19
Benny, Jack, *16*
Bergen, Edgar, and Charlie McCarthy, 10
Binion, Benny, 16, 19
Bolger, Ray, 10
Bonanza Motel and Casino, 18, *53*
Borge, Victor, 10
Boulder Dam, *see* Hoover Dam
Boulder City, Nevada, 118
Brewer, Teresa, 10
Burton, Lance, *41*

Caesars Palace, 10–11, *12, 13,* 17, 20, *57, 59, 61, 85*
Casino Legends Hall of Fame, *7, 35*
Castaways, 11, 17, 20
Chevalier, Maurice, 10
Chinatown Plaza, *107*
Circus Circus, 10, 18, *25, 31, 85*
Clark County Museum, *113*
Club Bingo, *14, 85*

Crawford, Cindy, 16
Crawford, Joan, 16
Crazy Girls, *80*

Desert Inn, 9–10, 17, 18, 21
Desert Rose Motel, 11
Diamond Inn, *107*
Dion, Celine, *59*
Dunes, 9, 10, 11, *12,* 17, 20, 49, *98*

El Rancho Vegas, *8,* 9, *14*
Elvis-A-Rama Museum, *107*
Excalibur, 11, *19, 21, 24, 31*

Flamingo and Fabulous Flamingo, 9, 11, *12,* 13, 16, 18, *61, 73*
Francis, Connie, 10
Frémont, John C., 7
Fremont Hotel and Casino, *89*
Fremont Street and the Fremont Street Experience, *4,* 7, *8,* 10, *75, 89, 92, 104*

Garland, Judy, *73*
Gere, Richard, 16
Golden Nugget, 18, 20, *103*
Grable, Betty, 16
Greenbaum, Gus, *83*
Greenspun, Hank, 8
Guardian Angel Cathedral, *79*
Guggenheim galleries, *71*

Hacienda Hotel and sign, 11, *25, 92*
Hammargren, Lonnie and "Lonnie's Castle," *113*
Harrah's, 63
Helldorado parade, *9*
Henderson, Nevada, 8, *113,* 114
Holiday Inn Boardwalk Hotel and Casino, 13, *45,* 63
Hoover Dam, 7, 18, 92, *113, 118*
Horseshoe Club, Binion's, *4,* 16
Hughes, Howard, 8, 16–17, 20, 21
Hull, Thomas, *8,* 9
Hyatt Resort at Lake Las Vegas, *114*

Imperial Palace, 15
International, 17

Kefauver, Estes, 16
Kennedy, John F., 13
Kennedy, Robert F., 16
Kerkorian, Kerkor "Kirk," 17–18, 21
King's Crown Tallyho Motel, 14

Knievel, Evil, 11

La Cage, An Evening with, *83*
La Concha Motel, *80*
Lake Las Vegas, *114*
Lake Mead, *118*
Landmark, 17
"Las Vegas," origin of name, 7, *128*
Las Vegas Motor Speedway, 19
Last Frontier Village, *104*
Laxalt, Paul, 17
Learning from Las Vegas, 13
Liberace and Liberace Museum, 18, *83, 111, 113*
Lied Discovery Children's Museum, *97*
Lone Palm Motel, 11
Luxor, 11, *19, 21, 24, 27*

Madame Tussaud's Wax Museum, *73, 75*
Mandalay Bay, 11, *21, 24*
Marina, 11, 18
Marino, Frank, *83*
Martin, Dean, 13, 17
MGM Grand (new), 11, 17–18, *39, 41, 53, 94*
MGM Grand (original), *see* Bally's
Midler, Bette, 16
Minsky, Harold, 10, 14
Mint, 18
Mirage, 11, 12, 18, 20, 21, 63, 64, 67, *98*
Money and the Power, The, 17, 21
Monorail, *75*
Monroe, Marilyn, *73*
Monte Carlo, 11, *41*
Moore, Demi, 16
Moore, Mary Tyler, 16
Mormons and Las Vegas Mormon Temple, 7, *97, 128*

Neiman, LeRoy, 7
Neon, Neon Museum, and neon boneyard, 7, *8,* 10, 13, *15, 16,* 18, 19, 20, 21, *35, 76, 83, 92, 97, 98, 103, 104*
Nevada Landing (in Jean, Nevada), *124*
New Frontier (originally Last Frontier), *8,* 13, 16–17, 18. 20, *107*
New York New York, 11, 18, *35, 39*
Newman, Paul, 16
Newton, Wayne, 14, *76*
No Limit, 19
Nuclear tests, 15

Old Las Vegas Mormon Fort State Historic Park, *128*

Palms, *98*
Paris Las Vegas, 11, *45, 49*
Picasso restaurant, 12
Pioneer Club, 8, *92*
Pocket Lounge, *103*
Prell, Milton, 13, 14, 20
Presley, Elvis, 14, 16, 17, *18, 19, 94, 107; also see* Elvis-A-Rama Museum
Pyramids Casino, *63*
"Rat Pack," The, 10, *17, 75*

Red Rock National Conservation Area, *123*
Reflection Bay Golf Club, *114*
Renoir's restaurant, 12, *67*
Rio, *98*
River Boat Casino, *63*
Riviera, 9, 13, 18, *80, 83*
Royal Nevada, *76*

Sahara, 9, 10, 13, *14,* 18, 19, *85*
Sands, 9, 10, 11, 17, *17,* 18, *75*
Sarno, Jay, *57*
Siegel, Benjamin "Bugsy," 16, *61, 73*
Siegfried and Roy, 63, 64
Silver Slipper, 17, *104*
Sinatra, Frank, 10, 13, 14, *17, 75*
Stardust, 9, 13, *76, 79*
Stratosphere, 19, *75, 86*
Streisand, Barbra, 17
Stupak, Bob, 19–20, *86*

Thomas, Danny, 10
Thornton, Billy Bob, 16
Treasure Island, 12, 18, 20, 21, *67, 98*
Tropicana, *4, 7,* 10, 13, *16, 31, 35*
Tropicana Motor Park, *94*
Trump, Donald, 14
Tumbleweed Casino, 8, *63*

Vegas Vic and Vegas Vicki signs, *8, 92*
Vegas World, 19, *86*
Venetian, 9, 11, 12, *71, 73*

Walters, Lou, 10
Weddings, 14, 15–16, 19, *19, 24, 94*
Wee Kirk o'the Heather Wedding Chapel, *94*
Weissmuller, Johnny, 16
Willis, Bruce, 16
Woodward, Joanne, 16
Wynn, Steve, 20–21, *49,* 63

Yablonsky, Joe, 16
Yashuda, Ginji, 14
Young Electric Sign Co. (YESCO), *103*